HOME for the HOLIDAYS

COLORING IN A WINTER WONDERLAND

Parragon

This edition published by Cottage Door Press, LLC, in 2020.
First published 2016 by Parragon Books, Ltd.

5005 Newport Drive, Rolling Meadows, Illinois 60008

Images used under license from Shutterstock.com and iStock.com
Cover illustration and interior artwork created by Clare Lloyd

ISBN: 978-1-68052-998-2

Printed in China

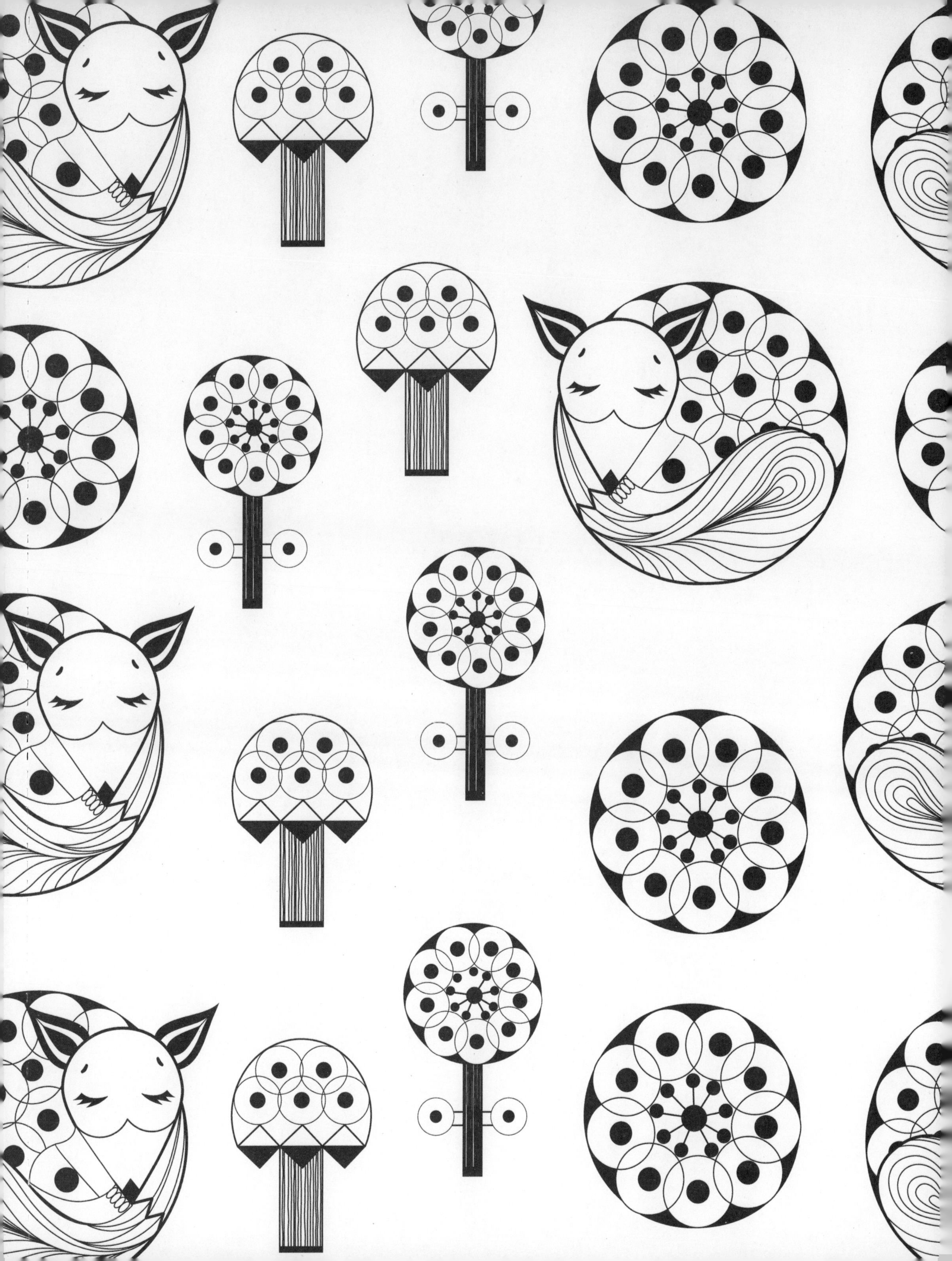

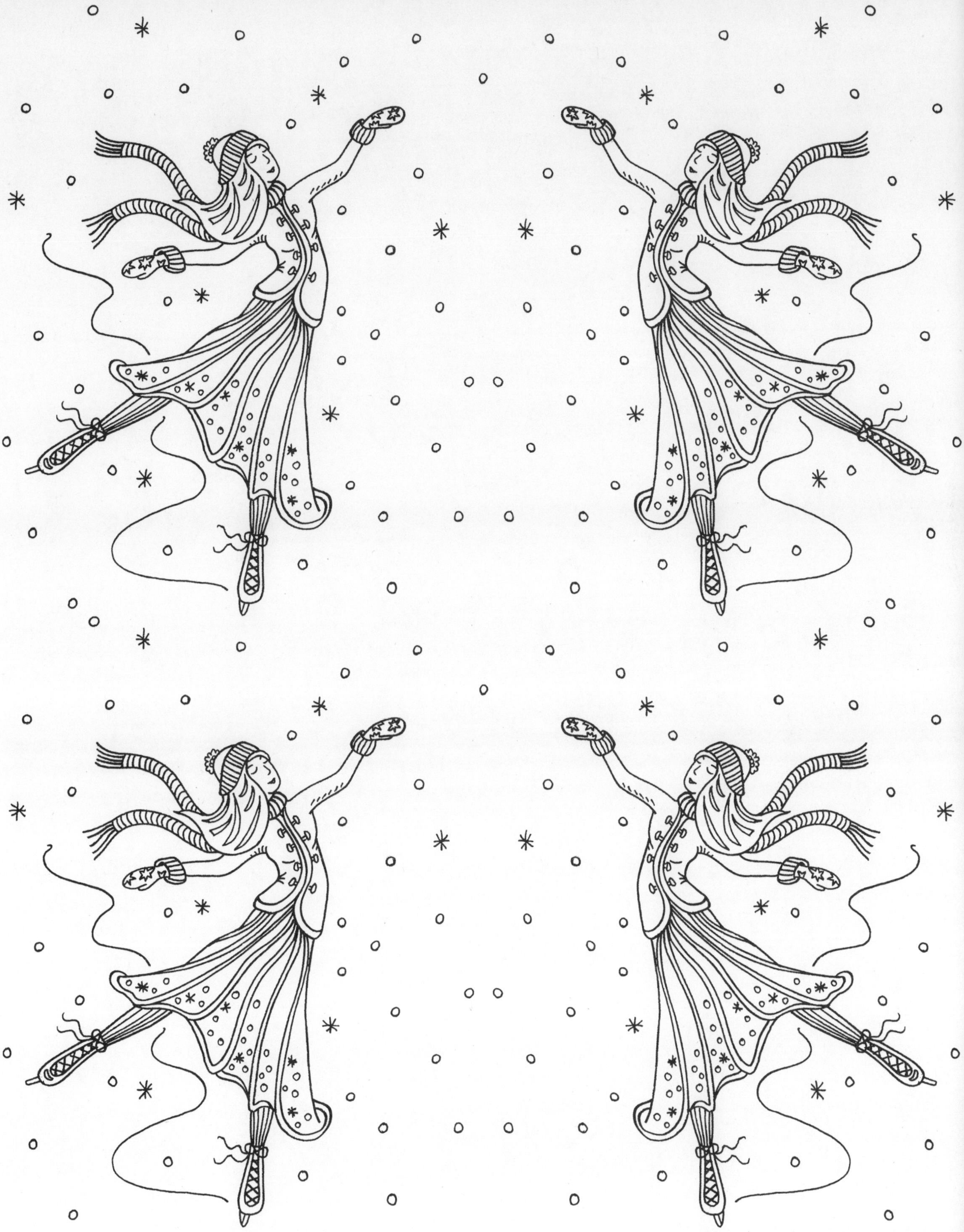

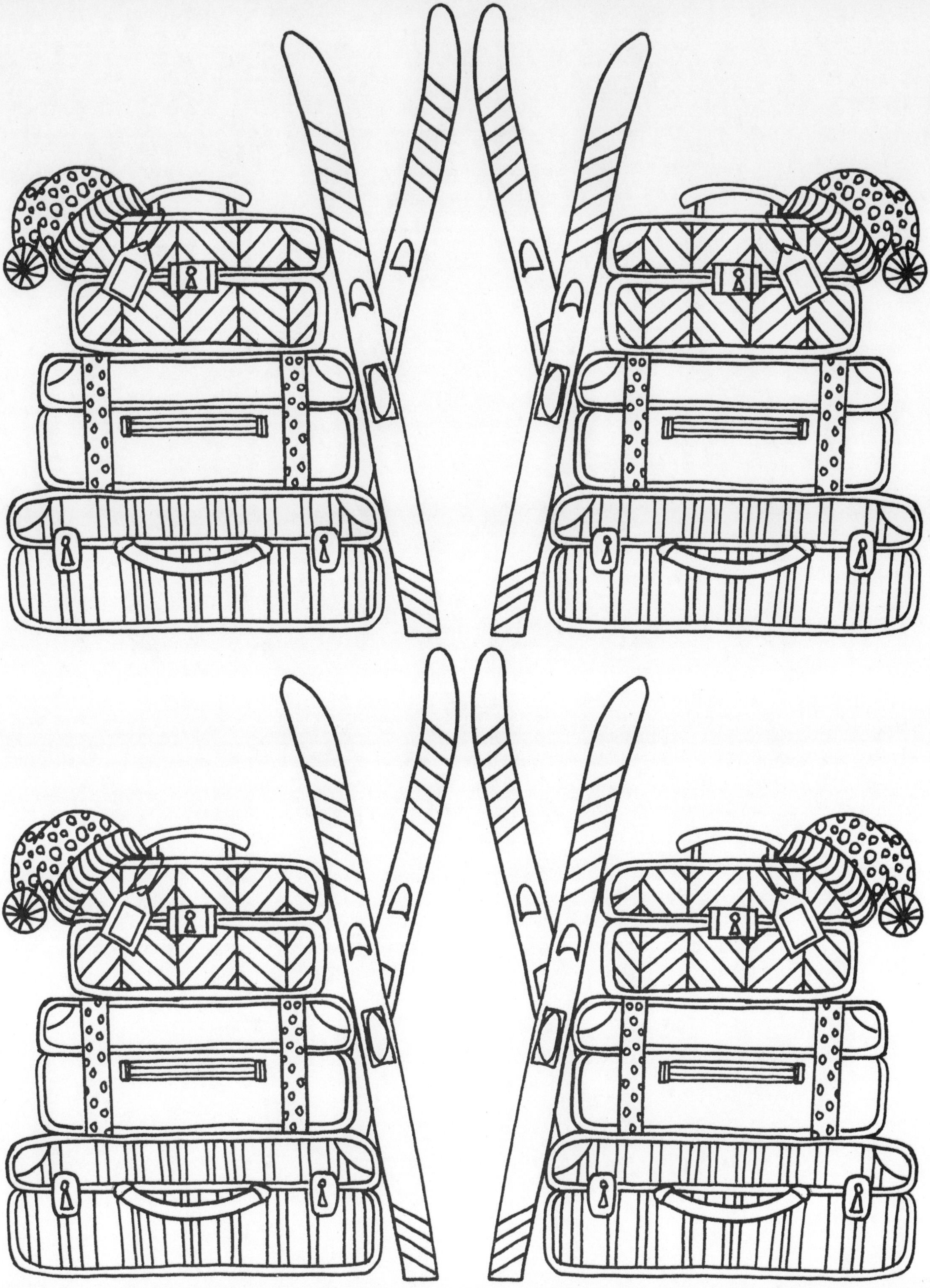

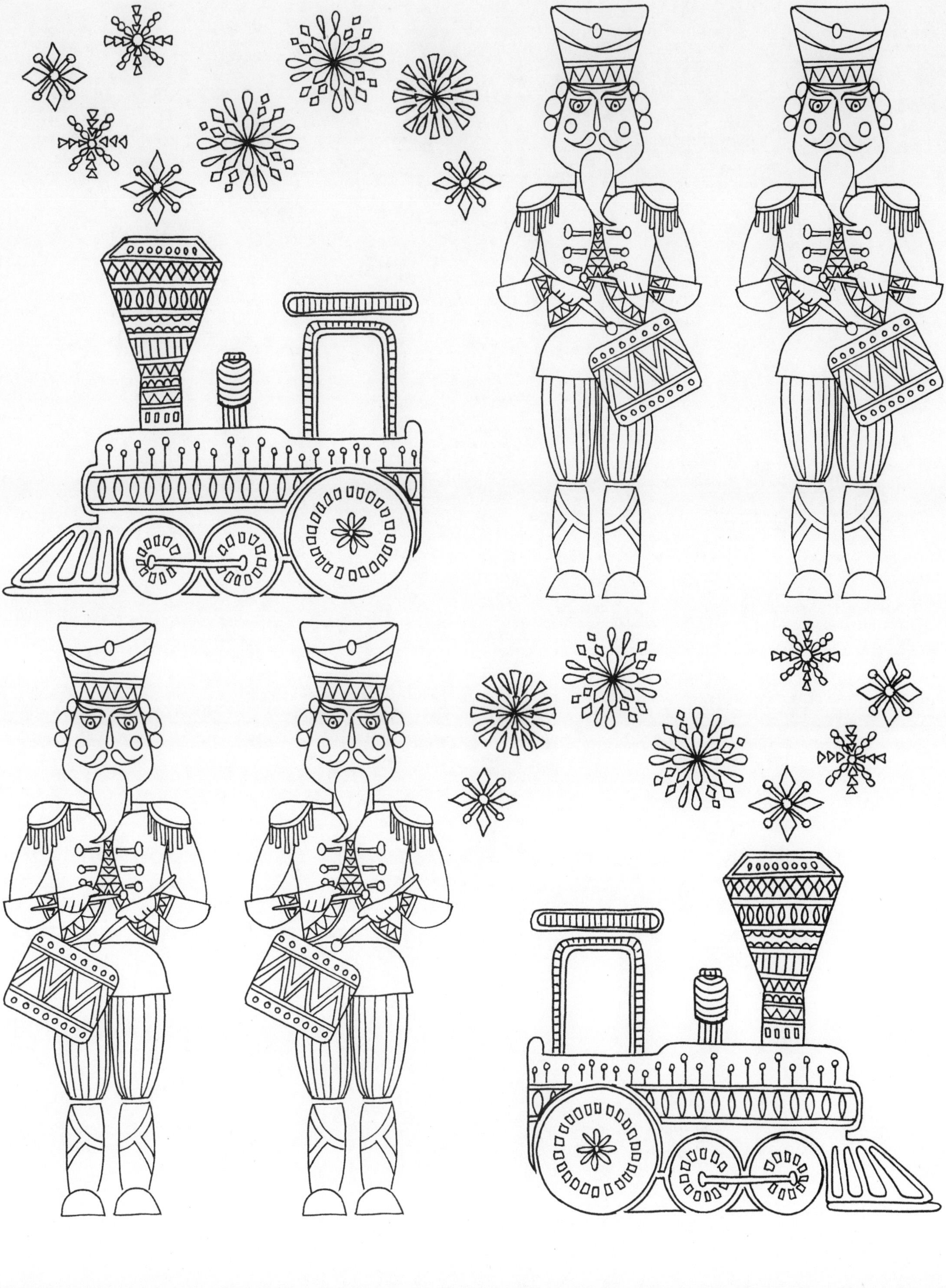